A Guide for Using

A Single Shard

in the Classroom

**Based on the novel written by
Linda Sue Park**

This guide written by **Melissa Hart, M.F.A.**

Teacher Created Materials, Inc.
6421 Industry Way
Westminster, CA 92683
www.teachercreated.com
©2003 Teacher Created Materials
Made in U.S.A.
ISBN 0-7439-3158-0

Edited by
Eric Migliaccio

Illustrated by
Megan Giles

Cover Art by
Kevin Barnes

Table of Contents

Introduction

A good book can enrich our life like a good friend. Fictional characters can inspire us and teach us about the world in which we live. We can turn to books for companionship, entertainment, and guidance. A truly beloved book may affect us forever.

Great care has been taken with Literature Units to select books that are sure to become your students' good friends.

Teachers who use this unit while reading *A Single Shard* will find the following features to supplement their own ideas:

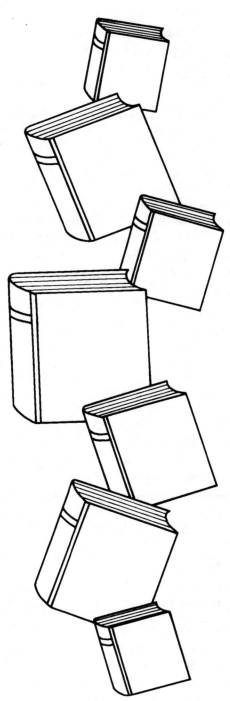

- Sample Lesson Plans

- Pre-reading Activities

- A Biographical Sketch and Picture of the Author

- A Book Summary

- Vocabulary Lists and Suggested Vocabulary Activities

- Chapters grouped for study with each section, including the following:

  —quizzes

  —hands-on projects

  —cooperative learning activities

  —cross-curricular connections

  —extensions into the reader's life

- Post-reading Activities

- Book Report Ideas

- Research Activities

- Culminating Activities

- Three Different Options for Unit Tests

- Bibliography

- Answer Key

We are certain this unit will be a valuable addition to your own curriculum ideas to supplement the novel *A Single Shard*.

Sample Lesson Plans

Each of the lessons suggested below can take from one to several days to complete.

Lesson 1
- Introduce and complete the pre-reading activities found on page 5.
- Read "About the Author" with your students (page 6).
- Read the book summary with your students (page 7).
- Introduce the vocabulary list for Section 1 (page 8).

Lesson 2
- Read chapters 1 and 2. As you read, place the vocabulary words in the context of the story and discuss their meanings.
- Administer the Section 1 quiz (page 10).
- Complete a vocabulary activity (page 9).
- Make clay (page 11).
- Explore animal symbols (page 12).
- Learn about Korea (page 13).
- Begin "Reading Response Journals" (page 14).
- Introduce the vocabulary lists for Section 2 (page 8).

Lesson 3
- Read chapters 3 and 4. As you read, place the vocabulary words in the context of the story and discuss their meanings.
- Administer the Section 2 quiz (page 15).
- Complete a vocabulary activity (page 9).
- Learn to whittle (page 16).
- Listen and learn about people (page 17).
- Investigate how to tell time without clocks (page 18).
- Observe your surroundings (page 19).
- Introduce the vocabulary lists for Section 3 (page 8).

Lesson 4
- Read chapters 5–7. As you read, place the vocabulary words in the context of the story and discuss their meanings.
- Administer the Section 3 quiz (page 20).
- Complete a vocabulary activity (page 9).
- Learn to weave mats (page 21).
- Write folk tales (page 22).
- Create inlay art (page 23).
- Explore tangible and intangible gifts (page 24).

- Introduce the vocabulary lists for Section 4 (page 8).

Lesson 5
- Read chapters 8–10. As you read, place the vocabulary words in the context of the story and discuss their meanings.
- Administer the Section 4 quiz (page 25).
- Complete a vocabulary activity (page 9).
- Make a map of students' routes from home to school (page 26).
- Design a Korean Market (page 27).
- Learn about Korea's invasions (page 28).
- Explore traditions and laws (page 29).
- Introduce the vocabulary lists for Section 5 (page 8).

Lesson 6
- Read chapters 11–13. As you read, place the vocabulary words in the context of the story and discuss their meanings.
- Administer the Section 5 quiz (page 30).
- Complete a vocabulary activity (page 9).
- Learn to use a pottery wheel (page 31).
- Explore ancient Korean roles (page 32).
- Create similes and metaphors (page 33).
- Investigate disappointments and opportunities (page 34).

Lesson 7
- Discuss questions your students may have about the novel (page 35).
- Assign book reports and research projects (pages 36–37).
- Begin work on culminating activities (pages 38–42).

Lesson 8
- Administer unit tests 1, 2, and/or 3 (pages 43–45).
- Discuss test answers and responses.
- Discuss the students' opinion of the book.
- Provide a list of related reading for students (page 46).

Lesson 9
- Celebrate the Korean day culminating activity (pages 38–42).

Before the Book

Before you begin reading *A Single Shard* with your students, you may find it beneficial for them to have an idea of the time period and cultural framework in which the book is set. Here are activities that might work well for your class.

1. Predict from the title what this story might be about.

2. Predict from the cover illustration what this story might be about.

3. Discuss what students know about Korea. Locate the country on a classroom map. Discuss the fact that Korea used to be one country but is now divided into communist North Korea and democratic South Korea.

4. Discuss what students know about pottery.

5. Download pictures of celadon pottery from the Internet or look at photos in an encyclopedia. Talk about how it differs from other pottery, particularly in terms of the glaze used.

6. Talk about the difficulties a 12-year-old child might have if he or she were an orphan.

7. Discuss the difference between tangible and intangible gifts. What might you give to someone if you wanted to be generous but didn't want to give an object? (Think in terms of services, time, an attentive ear, a smile, etc.)

8. Brainstorm the qualities that make a hero. (A hero doesn't necessarily have to be a strong person in a cape, provided he or she has other admirable characteristics.)

9. Answer these questions:

   Would you ever . . .

   ➤ live completely outdoors?

   ➤ work for free in order to learn a skill?

   ➤ work on a project until it is absolutely perfect?

   ➤ make a difficult journey to help a friend?

   ➤ pursue a goal no matter how difficult the pursuit became?

About the Author

Linda Sue Park is the daughter of Korean immigrants. Her father came to America after the Korean War. As a child growing up in Illinois, she loved to read. Some of her favorite books from childhood include *The Long Winter* by Laura Ingalls Wilder, *A Tree Grows in Brooklyn* by Betty Smith, and *Half Magic* by Edward Eager. She started writing poems and stories when she was four years old. When she was nine, she had a poem published in a 1969 edition of *Trailblazer Magazine*. The publisher paid her a dollar—which she gave to her father for Christmas.

Ms. Park had several other poems published in magazines while still in junior high and high school. She then attended Stanford University, where she competed for the gymnastics team. She earned a degree in English. After graduation, she worked as a public relations writer for an oil company.

Later, Ms. Park met and married a man from Ireland. They lived together in Dublin and London and had two children. Ms. Park taught English as a Second Language to college students and worked as a food journalist before moving with her family back to the United States in 1990.

In 1997, Ms. Park realized she wanted to write books for children. Her first book is titled *Seesaw Girl*. It was published in 1999. Her next book is titled *The Kite Fighters*. Ms. Park's father drew the illustrations at the beginning of each chapter of *The Kite Fighters*. *A Single Shard* is her third book. Published in 2001, it won the Newbery Medal in 2002. Her fourth book, published in 2002, is titled *When My Name Was Keoko*. Ms. Park also writes picture books for young children, as well as short fiction for adults.

She currently lives in New York with her family, a dog, and a hamster. She loves to cook, travel, and watch movies. She also likes to watch baseball and soccer and play board games.

When asked about what a writer can do to make his or her work the best it can be, Ms. Park said:

"Read. That's the single best thing an aspiring writer can do for his or her work. I once heard an editor say, 'Read a thousand books of the genre you're interested in. Then write yours.' I was astonished and pleased to hear her say this—because that's exactly what I did. During the years when I had no thought of writing for children, I read and read and read."

A Single Shard
By Linda Sue Park
(Clarion, 2001)

In the mid to late 12th century in a small village on the west coast of Korea, twelve-year-old Tree-ear has just come upon an unexpected gift of spilled rice grains. He shares the rice with his friend, Crane-man, in their home under a bridge. Tree-Ear is an orphan. He and Crane-man forage for food from other people's rubbish piles in the village of Ch'ulp'o. Such a life gives Tree-Ear plenty of time to watch the region's finest potter, Min, create beautiful celadon pottery.

One day, thinking no one is at home, Tree-ear examines Min's pottery. Suddenly, the potter comes up behind him. Tree-Ear drops and breaks several ceramic boxes. Min is furious. Tree-ear offers his assistance in order to make up for the broken boxes, and Min reluctantly accepts. Tree-ear hopes to learn how to throw pots on the pottery wheel, but Min puts him to work chopping wood for the kiln and digging up clay. During this time, Tree-ear receives lunch every day—and saves half of it for Crane-man at home under the bridge. Realizing this, Min's wife offers him more food. She also gives him a jacket and pants that once belonged to her son.

Then Tree-ear learns that a royal emissary is on tour to assign pottery commissions for the palace. The boy knows that Min wants a commission badly. He does all he can to help during the time that the master potter is preparing his pottery for the emissary's visit. He spies on a rival potter, Kang, and discovers a new technique involving inlaying patterns on pottery. This new style wins Kang a commission, but the emissary stops at Min's house and asks if he will incorporate the new inlay style into his own work. He asks Min to bring this new pottery to the palace in Songdo. Min explains that he is too old to make the journey to Songdo. Tree-ear offers to take Min's vases to the palace.

Crane-man makes a straw basket in which to carry the two new vases that Min has created for the palace. Min's wife gives Tree-ear food, and he sets off on the journey to Songdo. It is a long and dangerous trip. Just as Tree-ear is nearing his destination, tragedy strikes. He is faced with a difficult decision, and he risks both humiliation and failure to do what he believes is right.

Upon his return to Ch'ulp'o, Tree-ear faces more tragedy. However, he also discovers great joy. Thanks to his courage and honesty, he achieves his life's dream.

Vocabulary Lists

On this page are vocabulary lists that correspond to each sectional grouping of chapters. Vocabulary activity ideas can be found on page 9 of this book.

Section 1 (Chapters 1–2)

protruded	marrow	rutted
perusal	droning	precariously
glean	symmetry	disarray
oblivious	oaf(ish)	momentum
complied	emboldened	methodically
urchin	impudence	wincing
garner	derision	
arid	kiln	

Section 2 (Chapters 3–4)

dusk	toil	sludge
ministrations	brandishing	purified
frenzied	jabs	pummeling
culinary	inconvenience	patriarch
debt	deceiving	commission
curt	unobtrusive	meagerness
trundled	bland	
geometric	tedious	

Section 3 (Chapters 5–7)

garb	pantaloons	lotus
vigilance	tunic	commiserated
translucent	emissary	harangued
diversion	stealth	feigned
arduous	vessels	ferocity
plaited	impending	treacherously
ruefully	entourage	
tithe	makeshift	

Section 4 (Chapters 8–10)

noxious	endeavor	trudged
tumultuous	rifling	mock
serenity	foraging	lair
kinswomen	sincerity	courtiers
rashness	grudgingly	sovereign
perils	hospitality	impeccable
quaking	persimmons	
apprentices	mishap	

Section 5 (Chapters 11–13)

scrambling	shard	subside
quell	dignified	eddy
menacing	scrawny	girth
pallor	incredulous	bestowed
captor	skepticism	welter
throttling	clarity	medallions
pinioned	surreptitiously	
retched	barrage	

8

Vocabulary Activity Ideas

You can help your students learn the vocabulary words in *A Single Shard* by encouraging them to complete the stimulating vocabulary activities below.

- Ask your students to work in groups to create an illustrated book of the vocabulary words and their meanings.

- Separate students into groups. Use the vocabulary words to create crossword puzzles and word searches. Groups can trade puzzles with each other and complete.

- Play "Guess the Definition." One student writes down the correct definition of the vocabulary word. The others write down false definitions—though close enough to the original definition that their classmates might be fooled. Read all definitions, and then challenge students to guess the correct one. The students whose definitions mislead their classmates get a point for each student fooled.

- Use the word in five different sentences. Compare sentences and discuss.

- Write a short story using as many of the words as possible. Students may then read their stories in groups.

- Encourage your students to use each new vocabulary word in a conversation five times during one day. They can take notes on how and when the word was used, and then share their experience with the class.

- Play "Vocabulary Charades." Each student or group of students gets a word to act out. Other students must guess the word.

- Play "Vocabulary Pictures." Each student or group of students must draw a picture representing a word on the chalkboard or on paper. Other students must guess the word.

- Challenge students to a "Vocabulary Bee." In groups or separately, students must spell the word correctly, and give its proper definition.

- Talk about the different forms that a word may take. For instance, some words may function as more than one part of speech. The word "mock" is a good example of a word which can be both a verb and an adjective.

> You surely have many more ideas to add to this list. Try them! Practicing using selected words through the completion of creative activities increases student interest in and retention of vocabulary.

Quiz Time

Answer the following questions about Chapters 1 and 2.

1. Why is Tree-ear concerned about taking the rice from the ground?_____

_____

2. What does Crane-man tell Tree-ear about stealing? _____

_____

3. How did Tree-ear get his name? _____

_____

4. How did Crane-man get his name? _____

_____

5. How did Tree-ear come to live with Crane-man? _____

_____

_____

6. Why does Tree-ear enjoy watching Min? _____

_____

7. Describe the pottery Tree-ear sees outside Min's house. _____

_____

8. Why does Tree-ear offer to work for Min? _____

_____

9. Why is Tree-ear disappointed on his first day of work with Min? _____

_____

_____

10. Describe Tree-ear's experience of chopping wood for the kiln on his first day of work. _____

_____

_____

Making Clay

Potters in 15th-century Korea dug clay from the ground and shaped it into beautiful vases and ornamental boxes. Later, these pieces were glazed and fired. Clay has been used by almost every culture to form dishes and pots, as well as to create beads and other decorations. Outside Min's house, Tree-ear examines a ceramic duck which a painter would use to hold water for mixing ink.

> Tree-ear stared at Min's duck. Though it was now a dull gray, so detailed were its features that he found himself half listening for the sound of a quack. Min had shaped and then carved the clay to form curve of wing and tilt of head. Even the little tail curled up with an impudence that made Tree-ear smile.

Clay is a unique type of soil. Its particles are small. Some are one thousand times smaller than the particles found in sandy soil. Each particle can be coated with water, which helps the particles stick together.

Materials

- clay bed (easily found alongside a river or near a highway or house foundation—or even in the schoolyard!)
- water
- large coffee can
- shovel
- hammer
- newspapers
- sieve or piece of screen
- bowl
- old cloth
- airtight container

(Note to teacher: You may choose to use purchased clay from a craft store instead of digging for it.)

Directions

1. Fill a large coffee can with clean, clayey soil. If the soil is moist, set it out on newspapers in the sun.

2. Let it completely dry out. Then, remove twigs and rocks from the dry clumps of soil. Use a hammer to smash the clumps into powder.

3. Using a sieve (or screen), sift the powder back into the coffee can. Cover this powder with water. Add more water as it soaks in. Use your hands to break up lumps. Let the creamy mixture sit overnight.

4. The next day, pour off the extra water. Then line a bowl with an old cloth. Pour the wet clay into the bowl and let the clay dry out.

5. When the clay feels soft enough to handle easily, it's ready to mold into animals and other shapes. Store moist clay in an airtight container.

Animal Symbols

Animals have long been used as symbols in both life and literature. In *A Single Shard*, characters are named after animals. This is what Crane-man says about his name:

> When they saw my leg at birth, it was thought I would not survive. Then, as I went through life on one leg, it was said that I was like a crane. But besides standing on one leg, cranes are also a symbol of long life.

In groups of four, read through the pages suggested below. Then write down what each animal or insect symbolizes. Decide which animal best symbolizes you and explain your choice in a paragraph (below.) The chapter in which each animal or insect appears is given in parentheses.

Rabbit (3) Symbolizes: _____ _____	**Gnat** (4) Symbolizes: _____ _____
Lion (6) Symbolizes: _____ _____	**Dragon** (6) Symbolizes: _____ _____
Tortoise (6) Symbolizes: _____ _____	**Donkey** (7) Symbolizes: _____ _____
Tiger (7) Symbolizes: _____ _____	**Fox** (7) Symbolizes: _____ _____

Monkey (9)

Symbolizes: _____

_____

What animal or insect best symbolizes you? Explain your answer.

_____

_____

_____

_____

_____

Korea

Korea is a peninsula in Asia, southeast of China. Its history is rich with different foods, musical instruments, religions—and, of course, the celadon pottery that Tree-ear wants so badly to make.

Korea has also been marked by political unrest. Different countries have invaded this peninsula at different points in history. Nevertheless, Korea retains its culture and its pride as a distinct country.

Using an encyclopedia or the Internet, locate the following information about Korea.

Population: _____

Area in square miles or kilometers: _____

Capital city: _____

Neighboring countries: _____

_____

Most common religions: _____

_____

Common musical instruments: _____

_____

Common foods: _____

Korea is currently divided into two sections. What are their names? _____

_____

Songdo, to which Tree-ear eventually travels, is now called Kaesong. It served as the capital of Korea until 1392. Locate Kaesong on a map of the Korean peninsula.

Kaesong is bordered by which sea? _____

If you were to travel west from Kaesong, in what country would you eventually arrive?

_____

Where is the current capital city of Korea in relation to Kaesong (north, south, east, or west)?

_____

_____

Is Kaesong close to or far from the border that separates North and South Korea?

_____

Reading Response Journals

One way to ensure that the reading of *A Single Shard* becomes personal for each student is to include the use of Reading Response Journals in your lesson plan. Journal writing allows students to respond to the book in many ways. Here are some suggestions for the successful use of Reading Response Journals:

Explain to students that the purpose of the journal is to record their thoughts, ideas, observations, and questions as they read *A Single Shard*.

Provide students with, or ask them to suggest, topics from the story that stimulate writing. Here are examples from the chapters in Section 1:

➤ Tree-ear is an orphan. What particular challenges might he have to face because he has no parents?

➤ Min allows Tree-ear to work for him even when the boy has broken a precious ceramic box. Why do you think Min does this?

➤ Crane-man cares for Tree-ear as if he is his son. What actions does he take to let the reader know he cares deeply about Tree-ear?

➤ After reading each chapter, students may write about one or more discoveries they made about characters, plot, or setting.

➤ Ask students to draw responses to particular characters or events in the story, using blank pages in their journals.

➤ Tell students that they may pretend to be characters from the novel and record diary entries as such.

➤ Write down a quote from the novel and ask students to write a response to this quote. (They can summarize what they think the quote means both in the context of the book and in their own lives.)

➤ Allow students time to write in their journals daily, making sure to explain that entries will be read—but not graded—by the teacher. Credit is given for effort. If students must have a grade for the assignment, grade for the number of entries completed. Teachers may write non-judgmental notations to let students know that their journals are being read and enjoyed. Here are responses that will please and encourage young writers:

—"Your writing is so clear that I feel as if I am there."

—"You really understand this character [or plot, setting, or theme]."

—"I'd love for you to share this with the class. I think they'd enjoy it as much as I have."

Quiz Time

Answer the following questions about Chapters 3 and 4.

1. How does Tree-ear feel about chopping wood for Min each day? _____

   _____

2. What does Tree-ear notice about Min's wife's eyes? _____

   _____

3. Why does Tree-ear wish to continue working for Min? _____

   _____

4. Why is Tree-ear so excited when he realizes apprentices get a midday meal? _____

   _____

5. Why is Tree-ear ashamed when he sees Crane-man whittling a new crutch? _____

   _____

6. Why is Tree-ear's food bowl full again every evening? _____

   _____

7. Why do people prize celadon pottery so much? _____

   _____

   _____

8. What does Tree-ear learn about Min's work habits?_____

   _____

   _____

9. Why does Min want a royal commission so badly? _____

   _____

   _____

10. What might Tree-ear do to thank Min's wife for the extra food?_____

   _____

Soap Whittling

The term "to whittle" came about in 1552. It refers to the art of shaping a piece of wood or other object by cutting it with a knife. In chapter three, Crane-man whittles himself a new crutch after he breaks his old one against a rock. Some people whittle just to pass the time; others whittle beautiful art pieces such as walking sticks, totem poles, and even toothpicks!

Materials

For each student, you will need the following:

- paper and pencil
- a butter knife or wooden craft stick

- one bar of plain white soap
- old newspapers

Directions

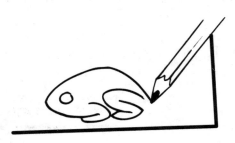

1. First, think about what shape you wish to create. Draw your shape on a piece of paper. Use a pencil so that you can erase if you make mistakes.

2. When you have decided on your shape, unwrap your bar of soap. Spread newspapers out on your work surface. Using a butter knife or wooden craft stick, begin to pare away the soap.

3. Make small, smooth strokes; don't try to hack into the soap with chopping motions. You can use toothpicks or the tip of a pencil to add small details to your shape.

4. Whittling takes a long time. It may take you several hours to create an object that pleases you. As you work, think about how much time it might have taken Crane-man to whittle an entire wooden crutch!

Listen and Learn

Tree-ear is an orphan with no social standing in the village of Ch'upl'o. Most people aren't even aware that he lives there.

> Skipping from one rubbish heap to the next, stopping at nearly every house in the village, listening to snatches of conversation along the road—in these ways Tree-ear had come to appreciate his lowly status, for people tended to ignore his presence entirely and on the rare occasions when they did notice him, usually spoke as if he weren't there.

Think about the people in your life that you seldom notice. Have you ever talked with these people? Do you know where they live, what they do, who their friends are, and what they want from life?

Separate into groups of three students each. Think about the people at your school whom you see every day but never talk to. This could be a younger schoolmate, a person who works in the cafeteria, or even the school principal! Make an appointment to interview this person (with your teacher's assistance, if necessary). Ask your chosen subject questions, then record his or her answers on the chart below. Finally, share your findings with the class.

	Tree-ear	_____ (name of your subject)
Where does he/she live?	under a bridge in Ch'ulp'o	
What does he/she like to do?	work with clay listen to stories	
Who are his/her friends?	Crane-man	
What does he/she want?	to learn to make pottery	
Other interesting details	He is honest, brave, and smart.	

Telling Time Without Clocks

In 12th-century Korea, people had no clocks or calendars. They had to rely on nature and handmade charts in order to tell what time it was, how long a period of time had passed, or in what direction they were traveling. Crane-man makes scratches under the bridge with a stone in order to chart Tree-ear's age. Tree-ear counts on his fingers to predict when Min will be working on a new pot. Later, he uses the moon to tell how long he has been working for Min.

It was two full moons now that Tree-ear had been working for Min, but it seemed like a year or even longer.

Using an encyclopedia or the Internet, answer the questions below.

1. What are the four phases of the moon called? _____
   _____

2. How long does it take the moon to complete an entire phase?_____

3. Tree-ear has been working for Min for two moons. How many months has he been working?
   _____

4. What is the North Star? _____

5. How did early travelers use the North Star so that they wouldn't lose their way on a journey?
   _____
   _____

6. What modern invention uses the directions north, south, east, and west in order to keep people from getting lost?_____

7. Who invented the first calendar? _____

8. How is this calendar different from the calendar you use?_____
   _____

9. What is an abacus? _____
   _____

10. What modern-day invention do people use in order to add, subtract, multiply, and divide?
    _____

11. What is a sundial? Draw a picture of one in the box to the right._____
    _____

12. How did sundials help people to tell time before there were clocks? _____
    _____

Observation

Tree-ear learns to observe his surroundings on his daily search for food.

> Tree-ear knew which mushrooms were tasty and which deadly. He knew the birds by their songs, and how a mountain lion's spoor looked different from that of a deer. And he never lost his way, for he knew where the streams were, pointing sure as an arrow back down the mountain toward the road.

Perhaps you walk or ride your bike to school every day. Even if you travel in a bus or a car, you can still observe your surroundings. On the back of this paper, write down all the things you can remember seeing on your way to school today.

It is interesting to find out the names of the trees and birds which thrive in your area of the country. A field guide is a book which can help you identify flora and fauna—that is, plants and animals—in your hometown. Using a field guide, an encyclopedia, or the Internet, answer the following questions.

- What is your state bird?_____
- What is your state tree? _____
- What is your state flower? _____
- List the names of three other birds that live in your area. Draw one in the box.

    1. _____
    2. _____
    3. _____

- List the names of three other trees that grow in your area. Draw one in the box.

    1. _____
    2. _____
    3. _____

- List the names of three other flowers that grow in your area. Draw one in the box.

    1. _____
    2. _____
    3. _____

Quiz Time

Answer the following questions about Chapters 5–7.

1. Why is Kang so concerned about hiding his pottery?_____

   _____

2. What type of pot does Tree-ear wish to make, and why?_____

   _____

3. Why is winter a problem for Tree-ear and Crane-man?_____

   _____

4. Why doesn't Tree-ear tell Min about Kang's new pottery technique?_____

   _____

   _____

5. How does Min react when Tree-ear hands him the flowering plum branches for his vases?

   _____

   _____

6. How does the emissary react to Min's work at the market?_____

   _____

7. Why does Min laugh when Tree-ear calls Kang's chrysanthemums "ugly"?_____

   _____

8. What strange thing occurs when Tree-ear is draining clay for Min's new pottery?_____

   _____

9. Why didn't Crane-man go to the temple to become a monk? _____

   _____

   _____

10. Why does Min smash his own vases? _____

   _____

Mat Weaving

Crane-man is a fine weaver. He weaves rice straw into mats and sandals. Later in the novel, he weaves an important container.

The art of weaving began more than 9,000 years ago. People wove grass, reeds, and even pine needles into baskets. In the years since the first weavers practiced this skill, people have used straw, gold, paper, and thread to create tapestries, clothing, and other beautiful objects.

You can see some of these pieces at the Metropolitan Museum of Art's website: *www.metmuseum.org.*

Click on the Antonio Ratti Textile Center and have fun exploring before you try your own hand at weaving!

Materials

- 9" x 13" (23 cm x 33 cm) pieces of colored paper, two per student

- scissors

- clear tape for edges, if needed

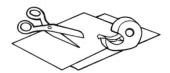

Directions

1. Use two different colors of paper. Cut one into strips 9" (23 cm) long and 1" (2.54 cm) wide.

2. Then cut slits in the other piece of paper, lengthwise, as shown in the diagram to the right. Make sure to leave an uncut border all the way around the second sheet of paper!

3. Weave the strips of paper in and out of the slits you have cut, following the diagram to the right.

4. When you have woven all the strips into your mat, you may tape the edges down or leave them as is. Now you have a piece of weaving to use as a placemat, book cover, or other decoration!

Folktales

Tree-ear grows up listening to Crane-man's folktales. These are stories about animals, as well as ones about the heroes and heroines of Korea. The dictionary defines a folktale as a story that is told orally among people. However, folktales may be written down, as well.

Work in groups of three or four. First, use a book or a search engine on the Internet to locate a folktale. Here is a list of people and creatures who figure prominently in some folktales.

Paul Bunyan	Johnny Appleseed	Kate Shelley
Pecos Bill	Jesse James	Ethan Allen
Coyote	Casey Jones	Raven
	Davy Crocket	

Now answer the questions below.

1. Who are the main characters in this folktale? _____

   _____

2. What is the setting of this story? _____

   _____

3. What is the conflict (the problem)? _____

   _____

4. How is this conflict resolved? _____

   _____

5. What is the message of this story (the theme)? _____

   _____

Finally, write your own group folktale on a separate sheet of paper. It should be at least a page in length. Answer the questions below for your own folktale.

1. Who are the main characters in this folktale? _____

   _____

2. What is the setting of this story? _____

   _____

3. What is the conflict? _____

   _____

4. How is this conflict resolved? _____

   _____

5. What is the message of this story? _____

   _____

The Art of Inlay

The inlay work with which Kang impressed the emissary and at which Min later excelled is both difficult and time-consuming.

Min used sharp tools with points of various sizes. The outline of the design was first etched lightly into the leather-hard clay with the finest point. Then Min would carve out the design a bit at a time… The glaze would collect in the crevices of the design, making it slightly darker than the rest of the surface.

You can get a feel for inlay work as you make the cookies below.

═══ Inlay Cookies ═══

Materials

- one batch of sugar cookie dough (recipe follows)
- several rolls of round, hard candies with a hole in the middle (colored candies—not mints)
- cookie sheets
- a rolling pin
- cookie cutters
- a spatula
- a butter knife or smaller, sharp knife

(Note to teacher: To save time, you may opt to purchase pre-mixed sugar cookie rolls in the refrigerated section of the market.)

Directions

1. Roll out the sugar cookie dough on a floured surface. Cut shapes into dough with cookie cutters and transfer the shapes onto a greased cookie sheet.
2. Now, trace a small shape in the middle of one cookie with the tip of your knife. This shape might be a diamond, square, circle, flower, or initial.
3. When you have traced a shape to your satisfaction, very carefully cut around it and gently lift it up off of the cookie with the tip of your knife. Discard this tiny piece of dough.
4. Now, select a candy from your roll. Place it in the middle of your inlay shape.
5. Bake the cookies, and then observe your edible piece of inlay art!

Sugar Cookie Dough

Ingredients

- $\frac{1}{2}$ cup (124 grams) soft butter
- $\frac{3}{4}$ cup (186 grams) packed brown sugar
- 2 beaten eggs
- $\frac{1}{2}$ tsp. (2 mL) vanilla extract
- $\frac{1}{2}$ tsp. (2 mL) lemon rind
- 1 cup (248 grams) whole wheat flour
- 1 cup (248 grams) white flour
- 2 tsp. (10 mL) baking powder
- $\frac{1}{4}$ tsp. (1 mL) salt

Directions

Cream together butter and sugar. Beat until light. Beat in eggs, vanilla, and lemon rind for 5 minutes. Set aside. Sift together dry ingredients. Add to first mixture. Mix well. Chill dough for an hour. Roll to $\frac{1}{4}$" (.63 cm). Cut into shapes and bake on a lightly greased tray for 10–12 minutes. Makes $4\frac{1}{2}$ dozen cookies.

Tangible and Intangible Gifts

A gift is something you offer to someone in order to show your affection. It can be something you can see, such as a toy, book, or item of clothing. This is a tangible gift. But gifts can also be intangible, such as time spent listening to someone or cheering him/her up with a joke. These gifts cannot be seen.

Think about the gifts that are given in *A Single Shard*. Some are listed on the chart below. Record who gives each gift, and who receives it. Then write down whether each gift is tangible or intangible. Discuss your answers with the class.

Gift	Giver	Recipient	Tangible	Intangible
woven sandals				
long hours of work				
a jacket and pants				
a bowl full of food				
a royal commission				
branches of flowering plum				
good advice				
a job				
cleaning a wound				
spilled rice				

Now think about one of your friends and/or family members. Make a list of three tangible gifts and three intangible gifts that you might give this person.

Tangible	Intangible
1.	1.
2.	2.
3.	3.

Quiz Time

Answer the following questions about Chapters 8–10.

1. What request does the emissary make of Min?_____

_____

2. What gift does Tree-ear realize he can give Min's wife? _____

_____

3. What does Min's wife do that surprises Tree-ear? _____

_____

4. What does Tree-ear learn about traditional potters and their sons? Why does this information hurt his feelings?

_____

_____

5. Why does Crane-man refuse Ajima's offer of food in exchange for work?_____

_____

6. Why does Crane-man laugh at Tree-ear? _____

_____

7. What advice does Crane-man give to Tree-ear before the boy leaves on his journey?

_____

_____

8. What animal does Tree-ear encounter on his journey? Why is this animal particularly significant?

_____

_____

9. How did the Rock of Falling Flowers get its name?_____

_____

10. Why do the bowls in Puyo's marketplace surprise Tree-ear? _____

_____

Making Maps

Tree-Ear did not have a map to use on his journey to Songdo. He most likely used the stars to tell him in which direction he was traveling. He also used landmarks (such as the town of Puyo) and locations (such as the Rock of Falling Flowers). Surely, his journey would have been easier if he'd had a map of the area.

Think about the route you take from home to school. What buildings do you pass? What unusual landmarks let you know that you are going in the right direction? Perhaps you pass a dog behind a fence every day, or a huge vegetable garden. Maybe you walk by or ride past a grocery store, a park, or a giant maple tree.

Draw a map of your route from home to school in the space below. Make sure to draw pictures of the landmarks you pass. Label them, as well. You may also include street names. Don't forget to draw pictures of your house and school.

The Korean Market

When Tree-ear enters the city gates of Puyo, he is surprised at how crowded the city is. The streets are narrow and full of people, oxen, and carts. Then he sees the market.

> On both sides of the street shop stalls were open... There were stalls that sold food and drink already prepared, and stalls that sold vegetables and fish for cooking at home. One stall sold nothing but sweets. There were bolts of fine silk, trays of gemstones, wooden toys. All manner of household goods could be had, baskets and straw sleeping mats and wooden chests.

Now, design a Korean market of your own.

Materials

- a six-foot (1.82 meters) piece of butcher paper, one for each group

- crayons or markers

- masking tape

Directions

1. Separate into groups of three or four. Choose one category from the box to the right. (Each group should choose a different category.) Using encyclopedias, books, or the Internet, research what types of products might have been included in your category.

2. Draw pictures of these items on your paper, making it look as though it is a market stall. Label your drawings. Finally, tape your paper up on the classroom wall. Each group should take turns explaining the different items it has "for sale."

Categories

vegetables

fruits

fish and meat

sweets

toys

clothing

woven items

furniture

jewelry

Korea's Many Invasions

The earliest known state in Korea was Old Choson, which was located in what is now northwestern Korea and southern China. Since the development of this first state, Korea has been conquered and invaded over and over by other countries. Crane-man tells Tree-ear the story of the "Rock of the Falling Flowers," about the invasion of the T'ang Chinese. He begins his story this way:

> "You know that our little land has suffered many invasions... The powers that surround us—China, Japan, the Mongols—have never left us in peace for long."

Using encyclopedias, books, or the Internet, answer the following questions.

1. Which country conquered Korea in around 108 B.C.? _____

2. What country invaded Korea in around 1231? _____

3. What country invaded Korea in around 1592? _____

4. What country ruled Korea between 1910 and 1945? _____

5. What two countries agreed to divide Korea at the 38th parallel for the purpose of accepting the surrender of Japanese troops in 1945? _____

6. Korea is now divided into two states. What are their names? _____

_____

Write a paragraph in the space below. Pretend you are a young person living in Korea at the time of one of the invasions. Describe what it is like to watch one of these other countries takes control of your homeland. Perhaps they try to change the way you eat, dress, or talk. Maybe they try to change your religion. How do you feel?

Laws and Traditions

Tree-ear is sad when Min cries, "You are not my son!" Crane-man explains that in Korea, sons of potters had to become potters themselves by decree of the king.

"I do not know if it is still a law," Crane-man continued, "But a well-kept tradition can be stronger than law."

A *law* is an action enforced by an authority, such as the court or police officers. A *tradition* is a customary pattern of thought, action, or behavior—not official, but suggested by society.

Think of some laws that govern your own life—for instance, the laws that prohibit us from injuring people. We have to stop our cars at red lights, and we're not allowed to just take cookies from the market shelf without paying for them. Write down five laws that you personally have to obey.

1. _____

2. _____

3. _____

4. _____

5. _____

Now think about traditions. In the United States (as well as in some other countries), women are traditionally married in a white dress. Many people traditionally enjoy a cake with candles on their birthdays. Holidays have traditions, including stockings at Christmas, a turkey dinner at Thanksgiving, and red envelopes full of money during Japanese New Year. Write down five traditions that you follow.

1. _____

2. _____

3. _____

4. _____

5. _____

Think once more about the Korean tradition that says that because Tree-ear is not his son, Min is not allowed to teach the boy to make pottery. What do you think about this? Should the tradition be changed, or should it stay the same? Explain your answer in the space below.

_____

_____

_____

_____

_____

Quiz Time

Answer the following questions about Chapters 11–13.

1. What do the two men at the Rock of the Falling Flowers want from Tree-ear?_____

    _____

2. Why does Tree-ear think about jumping off the edge of the cliff?_____

    _____

3. How does Tree-ear protect the shard of Min's pottery before he takes it to Songdo?

    _____

    _____

4. Why is Tree-ear briefly distracted when he arrives in Songdo? _____

    _____

5. What do the guards and the official think of Tree-ear when he arrives outside the palace?

    _____

    _____

6. Why does emissary Kim award a commission to Min after seeing just a single shard of his
    pottery? _____

    _____

7. Why are Ajima and Min strangely quiet when Tree-ear returns to his village?_____

    _____

8. How did Crane-man die?_____

    _____

9. What two things do Ajima and Min offer Tree-ear?_____

    _____

10. Who do you think made the "Thousand Cranes" vase described at the end of this book? Explain
    your answer._____

    _____

Fun with the Pottery Wheel

The potter's wheel was invented around 400 B.C. It consists of a flat disc that revolves horizontally around a pivot. The potter begins by placing a lump of clay into the center of the wheel. Then he/she pulls the clay into a cylinder and inserts one thumb into the top. The potter pulls up the sides of the piece and shapes the bowl or vase until it is satisfactory. Finally, the potter removes the piece from the wheel by running a thin wire underneath it. The piece is then fired in a kiln—much like Min's oven for which Tree-ear was forever gathering wood.

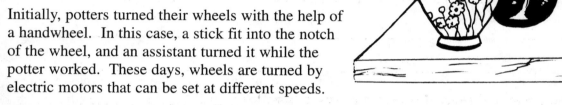

Initially, potters turned their wheels with the help of a handwheel. In this case, a stick fit into the notch of the wheel, and an assistant turned it while the potter worked. These days, wheels are turned by electric motors that can be set at different speeds.

Now, see if you have the patience to be a potter yourself!

Materials

- clay (purchased from a craft or toy store)

- bowl of water

- a potter's wheel

Directions

1. Place a lump of clay in the center of the wheel. Turn on the motor, and form your lump into a cylinder. You may use a little water if they clay begins to dry.

2. When your cylinder is formed, stick one thumb into the top of it, and begin to widen the hole, pulling up the sides of your vase or pot as the wheel turns. Your goal is to create a well-formed, smooth piece.

3. You may choose to fire your creation in a kiln or set it out in the sun to dry.

Note to teachers: Some schools have a pottery wheel available through their art department. Small, inexpensive wheels are available in the art section of toy or craft stores. You can also ask for demonstrations and assistance from potters at your local community college or art center.

Ancient Korean Roles

A role is an expected behavior based on an individual's position in society. In *A Single Shard*, there are several characters who play different roles. Some roles have to do with power. Emissary Kim plays a very important role in the lives of others, as he has the power to give commissions to people such as Min. Min's role as a potter requires him to work hard and take on an apprentice. Typically, this apprentice would be his son. Although Min doesn't have as much power as Emissary Kim, he is respected among the potters in Ch'ulp'o. Tree-ear, because he is an orphan, has a very different sort of role. Most people in his village don't even notice him, much less respect him. Until he begins working for Min, he must eat food from other people's rubbish heaps and sleep under the bridge.

Here is a list of different social roles found in 12th-century Korea:

> orphan   > apprentice   > craftsperson (potter,
                                                       calligrapher, weaver, etc.)
> monk   > emissary

Separate into groups of five. Each person in your group should assume one of the roles above. Using an encyclopedia, books, or the Internet, answer the questions below regarding your role in 12th century Korea. Then share your findings with your group.

1. What is your role in society?_____

   _____

2. How do other people in the society view you? _____

   _____

3. Where do you live? _____

   _____

4. How do you get food? _____

   _____

5. How do you spend your time?_____

   _____

6. Do you work for someone, or does someone work for you? _____

   _____

7. What are the benefits of your role?_____

   _____

8. What are the problems with your role?_____

9. On a blank sheet of paper, draw a picture of yourself in your role.

10. Would you like a different role? If so, how could you obtain it? _____

    _____

Similes and Metaphors

Figurative language is language that compares one thing with another in order to make it come alive for the reader. This type of language includes similes and metaphors.

➤ A simile compares one thing to another using the words "like" or "as." For instance, in *A Single Shard*, Crane-man says about Tree-ear, "'You clung to my good leg like a monkey to a tree.'" He compares Tree-ear to a monkey in order to help the reader see the action more precisely.

➤ A metaphor compares two things without using the words "like" or "as." Tree-ear says this about the robber at the Rock of the Falling Flowers: "Silently he swore to himself that this dog of a man would never win the jiggeh with its priceless contents."

The robber is compared to a dog. This explains Tree-ear's negative feelings about the man. Linda Sue Park uses many similes and metaphors in *A Single Shard*. Read the ones below. Write down what is being compared and what the author wishes to explain with this comparison.

Similes

"The thought broke through Tree-ear's fatigue like a shaft of sunlight piercing a cloud." (page 33)

- What is being compared? _____
- What is explained by this comparison? _____

"His frustration at the meagerness of his thanks was like the small but constant whine of a gnat in his thoughts." (page 48)

- What is being compared? _____
- What is explained by this comparison? _____

"As he walked home that evening, no answer surfaced among the questions that darted about like fish in his mind." (page 51)

- What is being compared? _____
- What is explained by this comparison? _____

Metaphors

"On his way to Min's house early one morning, as the plum trees took on their gold and scarlet autumn garb, Tree-ear spied the potter Kang wheeling a cart toward the kiln site." (page 49)

- What is being compared? _____
- What is explained by this comparison? _____

"'This scrawny scarecrow of a child claims a royal appointment?'" (page 133)

- What is being compared? _____
- What is explained by this comparison? _____

"There were some things that could not be molded into words." (page 139)

- What is being compared? _____
- What is explained by this comparison? _____

Shut Door, Open Door

Tree-ear has to endure many hardships in *A Single Shard*. To begin with, he is an orphan. Then he breaks one of Min's pots. Tradition dictates that he cannot be a potter, as he is not Min's son. Then he makes a journey to Songdo and meets with disaster. However, Tree-ear does eventually triumph. As Crane-man says, "'My friend, the same wind that blows one door shut often blows another open.'" He means that even when life looks impossible, a gift of some sort is waiting!

Think about the events in Tree-ear's life, as listed below. Beside each "shut door" event, write the "open door" event that occurs as a result.

Shut Door	Open Door
1. Tree-ear is orphaned, and the monks will not take him in, as there is illness in the monastery.	1. _____ _____
2. Min surprises Tree-ear outside his house, and Tree-ear breaks one of the potter's boxes.	2. _____ _____
3. A wild animal eats the food Tree-ear had been saving for Crane-man.	3. _____ _____
4. Min initially refuses to teach Tree-ear to make pottery.	4. _____ _____
5. Robbers smash both of the vases Tree-ear had hoped to take to Songdo.	5. _____
6. Tree-man returns to his village to find that Crane-man has died.	6. _____ _____

Now, think of three "shut door, open door" events from your own life. Write them below.

Shut Door	Open Door
1. _____ _____	1. _____ _____
2. _____ _____	2. _____ _____
3. _____ _____	3. _____ _____

Any Questions?

When you finished reading *A Single Shard*, you most likely had questions that were left unanswered. Write them in the space below.

1. _____

_____

2. _____

_____

3. _____

_____

Now, work in groups or by yourself to write down possible answers for the questions you wrote above, as well as those printed below. Share your answers with your class.

- Does Tree-ear eventually find his parents? _____
- Does he ever return to Songdo? _____
- Does Tree-ear become a famous potter? _____
- Does he receive a commission from Emissary Kim? _____
- Does Tree-ear ever get married? _____
- Does he have a son, and does he train that son to be a potter? _____
- What happens to Min? _____

_____

- What happens to Kang, who received a limited commission from Emissary Kim?

_____

_____

- Does tradition change so that children who don't have potters for fathers can still learn the art of making pottery? _____

_____

- Does Tree-ear adopt an orphan? _____

_____

- Does Tree-ear live in the village of Ch'ulp'o all his life? _____
- Are the robbers who smash Min's pots ever caught? _____
- Does Tree-ear develop a new technique that all the potters eventually copy?

_____

_____

- What happens to Ajima? _____

_____

- Is Korea invaded again? _____

_____

- What types of pots does Tree-ear make? _____

_____

Book Report Ideas

There are several ways to report on a book after you have read it. When you have finished *A Single Shard*, choose a method of reporting from the list below, or come up with your own idea on how best to report on this book.

✤ Make a Book Jacket

Design a book jacket for this book. On the front, draw a picture that you feel best captures this story. On the back, write a paragraph or two which summarizes the main points of this book.

✤ Make a Time Line

On paper, create a time line to show the significant events in Tree-ear's life. You may illustrate your time line, if you wish.

✤ Design a Scrapbook

Use magazine pictures, photographs, and other illustrations to create a scrapbook that Tree-ear might keep to document his life with Min and Ajima. He might choose to decorate his scrapbook with stickers or to include a letter to Crane-man. He might also include pictures of his new friends or a picture of one of his pots.

✤ Make a Collage

Using old magazines and photographs, design a collage that illustrates all of Tree-ear's adventures in *A Single Shard*.

✤ Create a Time Capsule

What items might Tree-ear put in a time capsule by which to have his life remembered? What container might he use as a time capsule?

✤ Write a Biography

Do research to find out about the life of Linda Sue Park. You may use the Internet (she has her own website at *www.lindasuepark.com*) or magazines. Write a biography, showing how Ms. Park's experiences might have influenced her writing.

✤ Act Out a Play

With one or two other students, write a play featuring some of the characters in this novel. Then act out your play for your class.

✤ Design a Diorama

Using a shoebox as a frame, create a diorama that illustrates an important scene in the novel. You may use all sorts of materials (paper, sand, clay, paint, fabric, etc.) to bring this scene to life.

✤ Make Puppets

Using a variety of materials, design puppets to represent one or all of the characters in this novel. You may decide to work with other students to write and perform a puppet show.

Research Ideas

As you read *A Single Shard*, you discovered geographical locations, events, and people that you might wish to know more about. To increase your understanding of the characters, places, and events in this novel, do research to find out more information.

Work alone or in groups to find out more about one or more of the items listed below. You may use books, magazines, and the Internet to do your research. Afterwards, share your findings with the class.

✛ orphans
✛ celadon pottery
✛ monks
✛ rice cakes
✛ weaving
✛ other countries in the 12th century
✛ trees and plants in Korea
✛ birds and animals in Korea
✛ the homeless
✛ Korean clothing from the 12th century
✛ Korean marketplaces
✛ villages vs. towns
✛ throwing pots

✛ Songdo (now called Kaesong)
✛ invasions of Korea
✛ contemporary Korea
✛ 12th century Korean houses
✛ 12th century Korean transportation
✛ calligraphy
✛ Korean food
✛ Korean folk tales
✛ China's influence on Korea
✛ Japan's influence on Korea
✛ Korean music
✛ Korean palaces and temples
✛ master/apprentice relationships
✛ Korean New Year
✛ communist North Korea

Korean Day

After reading *A Single Shard*, perhaps you wondered what it was like to live in 12th-century Korea. That was 800 years ago. At that time, there was no television, no cars, no radio, no pizza or hamburgers—few of the elements that make up today's culture. But as the story of Tree-ear proves, life was still interesting!

Work together as a class to plan a Korean Day celebration. You may choose to focus on contemporary North or South Korean culture; or you may, in the spirit of *A Single Shard*, focus on 12th-century Korean culture. Perhaps you will want to invite parents and/or other classes to participate in your celebration. To invite other people to your party, use the invitations on page 39.

Here are some ideas for ways in which you can make your Korean Day celebration both special and educational.

➤ Wear costumes that reflect the culture.

➤ Wear your hair in a style that reflects the culture.

➤ Cook foods from Korea, including rice cakes and the other recipes on page 40.

➤ Make examples of Korean pottery (page 31) or of clay sculptures (page 11).

➤ Weave placemats (page 21) for guests to eat off of.

➤ Display your Korean market (page 27).

➤ Display a map of Korea, with Songdo (now called Kaesong) labeled.

➤ Set up a storytelling corner and tell folktales (page 22).

➤ Make a display illustrating what you learned about ancient Korean roles (page 32).

➤ Create a time line showing the highlights of Korean history.

➤ Play the Yut game (page 42).

➤ Set up a pottery wheel or set out clay so that your guests may learn to make pots and/or vases.

➤ Draw pictures of flowering plum blossoms (you can see pictures of them in a tree identification book), such as the ones Tree-ear wanted to put in a prunus vase, and display them on the walls.

➤ Set up a reading and research center with books about Korea and pottery (see Bibliography).

➤ Make Inlay Cookies (page 23).

➤ Post your "Door Shut/Door Open" pages on a bulletin board for guests to read.

Korean Day *(cont.)*

Students should color and write on the invitation below to invite guests to Korean Day. Duplicate as many copies of this page as needed. Then cut around the border.

You're invited!

What: _____

_____

Who: _____

_____

When: _____

_____

Where: _____

_____

Why: _____

_____

Korean Cooking

Ajima packs deok (rice cakes) for Tree-ear's long journey to Songdo. Rice cakes have long been a part of Korean traditional food. People make them for celebrations or for periods of mourning. The color, shape, and content of these cakes vary from person to person. Often, a group of neighbors will share rice cakes with one another to indicate their feelings of kindness.

Rice Cakes

Glutinous rice, also known as sweet rice, is reserved in Asia for special occasions—many times for sweets. This rice is dense and gummy. It is found in Asian markets.

Materials

- large bowl
- food processor
- flat kitchen towel (not Turkish weave)
- large pot with lid
- perforated steamer tray

Ingredients

- 3 cups (720 grams) glutinous rice
- 2 teaspoons (10 mL) salt
- $^1/_4$ cup (60 mL) sugar

Directions

Rinse the rice well. Cover with cold water and soak for at least 12 hours. Drain well and grind in a food processor. Add salt and sugar as you grind, creating a dense, sticky paste.

Wrap a wet kitchen towel over and around a perforated steamer tray. Prepare a cake on the towel by patting down the glutinous rice. Cover the steamer tightly and steam for 45 minutes to an hour. Test with a toothpick: if the toothpick emerges dry, then the cake is done. Lift out the cake in the towel and carefully turn it upside down on a cutting board. Allow the cake to cool somewhat, then slice it into sections while it is still warm. Serve immediately. Makes 24 small cakes.

Fruit Leather

Ajima also packs *gokkam* (sweet, dried persimmons), which Tree-ear loves. Dried fruit is widely available at your local market. Fruit leather is a fun way to make use of this dried fruit on a hiking trip. Traditionally, peaches and apricots are used, but you can use any type of dried fruit for the recipe below.

Materials

- food processor
- cutting board
- airtight container
- rolling pin

Ingredients

- 1 pound (450 grams) dried apricots
- $^1/_2$ pound (225 grams) dried peaches
- $^1/_4$–$^1/_2$ cup (60–120 grams) sugar

Directions

Finely chop the apricots and peaches together in a food processor. Liberally sprinkle a board with sugar. Pat and roll out the fruit mixture to $^1/_8$" (.31 cm) thick. Cut into $1^1/_4$" (3.17 cm) x 2" (5 cm) strips. Roll each strip lengthwise into a tight roll. Makes $1^1/_2$ pounds. Stored in an airtight container, fruit leather keeps well at room temperature for several months.

12th-Century Korean Clothing

The traditional Korean costume was divided into a top and a bottom. Women wore both pants and skirts. The color of one's clothing said much about social class. Yellow was reserved for royal clothing. It is likely that the king in his Songdo palace wore a yellow jacket and pants. White symbolized modesty. Most people wore this color.

Men's and women's clothing from 12th-century Korea is depicted below. You may choose to color these pictures or create an outfit similar to them for your Korean Day celebration.

Korean Games

Korean children like to fly kites, spin tops, and slide on the snow during Korean New Year celebrations. But the most popular game to play on Korea's New Year's Day is the Yut game. Yut became popular in the first century, and it has been played in Korea ever since. Here is a modified version of the Yut game, which you may choose to play at your Korean Day celebration.

Materials

- the Yut game has four sticks that look like the picture to right:

  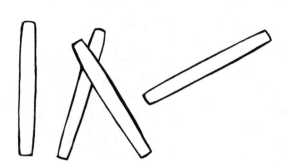

  The flat part of the stick is the rear. The curved part with the drawing is the front. The sticks are thrown into the air and examined carefully after they have fallen down. Sticks must be the same size, shape, and weight. You may draw a decoration on one side of four craft sticks to simulate Yut sticks.

- one copy of the Yut Pan below, enlarged and printed on a separate sheet of paper.

- one marker for each student (pebbles work well, as do coins)

Directions

The patterns into which the sticks land are named after farm animals. Here is a legend to help you play the Yut game:

➤ One stick upside down = *do* (pig)   ➤ Two sticks upside down = *gye* (dog)

➤ Three sticks upside down = *geol* (sheep)   ➤ Four sticks upside down = *yut* (cow).

➤ Four sticks right-side up = *mo* (horse)

Each player starts in the exact center of the Yut Pan. Choose a player to throw the sticks first. Determine which pattern the sticks have fallen into. *Do* advances 1 space, *gye* 2 spaces, *geol* 3 spaces, *yut* 4 spaces, and *mo* 5 spaces.

Yut Pan

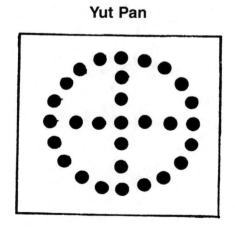

The first player moves his/her marker down one spoke of the Yut Pan. The number of spaces moved is indicated by the pattern of the sticks. Then the next player gets a turn. The goal is to move out into the circle, all the way around (clockwise), and back into the center of the circle before any other player.

Objective Test and Essay

Matching: Match the descriptions of the characters and places with their names.

Tree-ear	Min	Kang	Ch'ulp'o
Crane-man	Ajima	Emissary Kim	Songdo

1. Grants much-desired commissions to artists around the country _____

2. Takes a great deal of time creating extraordinary pots _____

3. Village in which Min and Ajima live _____

4. Gives Tree-ear good advice and weaves sandals_____

5. Gives Tree-ear enough food for both him and his friend _____

6. Location of the palace in which Emissary Kim works _____

7. First potter in Ch'ulp'o to make use of the inlay technique _____

8. Makes a dangerous journey to help his master _____

True or False: Answer **True** or **False** in the blanks below.

_____ 1. Min agrees immediately to teach Tree-ear to make pottery.

_____ 2. Crane-man doesn't become a monk because he sees a fox.

_____ 3. Ajima gives Tree-ear her dead son's clothing.

_____ 4. Emissary Kim gives Kang a permanent commission.

_____ 5. Tree-ear tells Min about Kang's new inlay technique.

Short Answer: Write a brief response to each question in the space provided.

1. How did Tree-ear find food before he worked for Min?_____

_____

2. What do the other potters in Ch'ulp'o say about Min and his work? _____

_____

3. Name the two animals that Tree-ear makes out of clay. _____

_____

4. How does Tree-ear persuade Emissary Kim to give Min a royal commission?_____

_____

5. Describe the prunus vase that is mentioned at the end of *A Single Shard.*_____

_____

Essay: Respond to the following on a separate piece of paper.
Courage is an important theme in *A Single Shard*. Min's wife, Ajima, shows courage when she begins to provide food and clothing for Tree-ear even though she still may be grieving for her dead son. Other characters show equal courage. In an essay, explain how Tree-ear, Crane-man, and Min show courage, each in his different way. Include in your essay your definition of the word "courage."

Response

Explain the meaning of these quotations from *A Single Shard*. (Note to teacher: Choose the appropriate number of quotes to which your students should respond.)

Chapter 1: "'Good deserves good, urchin. The rice on the ground is yours if you can be troubled to gather it.'"

Chapter 1: "'Scholars read the great words of the world. But you and I must learn to read the world itself.'"

Chapter 2: "'I would not steal. Stealing and begging make a man no better than a dog.'"

Chapter 3: "Tree-ear's joy at being forgiven was like a wisp of smoke; Min's orders for the day blew it into nothingness."

Chapter 3: "Of one thing he was certain: The feast-day banquets in the palace of the King could never better the modest meal before him, for he had earned it."

Chapter 4: "'You are like the ears of a scrawny little tree, noticed by none but hearing all!'"

Chapter 4: "His frustration at the meagerness of his thanks was like the small but constant whine of a gnat in his thoughts."

Chapter 5: "'How can you work properly for the honorable potter if you are shivering with cold?'"

Chapter 6: "Listening, saying little, his eyes half-closed and a half-smile on his face, Kang looked like nothing so much as a man with a secret."

Chapter 6: "'I knew this jug could be by no other than the same man who made that pot.'"

Chapter 7: "'Between the fox and you, I was destined never to become a monk!'"

Chapter 7: "The dreaded brown tint suffused the glaze of every piece; some of them were marred with brown spots as well."

Chapter 8: "'But if you were to produce something using this inlay style, and bring it to me in Songdo, I would guarantee a careful consideration of the work.'"

Chapter 8: "Min choked out the last words: 'You are not my son.'"

Chapter 9: "'He does not wish to be fed out of pity.'"

Chapter 10: "He had slept for who knew how long, with a fox nearby—and he had survived!"

Chapter 11: "He had made up his mind: he would journey on to Songdo and show the emissary the single shard."

Chapter 12: "'How is it that a commission can be awarded without seeing the work?'"

Chapter 13: "'When they pulled him from the river, he was clutching this in his hand.'"

Chapter 13: "One day at a time, he would journey through the years until he came upon the perfect design."

Conversations

Work in size-appropriate groups to write and perform the conversations that might have occurred in one of the following situations. If you prefer, you may use your own conversation idea for characters from *A Single Shard*.

- Tree-ear and Ajima talk about her dead son. (2 persons)

- Min and Kang talk about the new inlay technique that both men are using. (2 persons)

- Emissary Kim talks to the king about Min's pottery. (2 persons)

- Crane-man talks to Min and Ajima about Tree-ear's desire to become a potter. (3 persons)

- Crane-man and Tree-ear talk about Crane-man's childhood. (2 persons)

- Ajima and Min talk about adopting Tree-ear. (2 persons)

- The robbers see Tree-ear and plan how best to rob him. (2 persons)

- Crane-man does work around the house and yard for Ajima. (2 persons)

- Tree-ear, Crane-man, Min, and Ajima celebrate the Korean New Year together. (4 persons)

- Min teaches Tree-ear to throw a pot. (2 persons)

- Ajima talks to one of the village women about her husband. (2 persons)

- Kang talks to Tree-ear about Min's royal commission. (2 persons)

- Min, Ajima, and Tree-ear have dinner together the first night the boy lives with them. (3 persons)

- Tree-ear talks about Min with the other apprentices. (3–4 persons)

- Min talks to Ajima about wanting a partial commission. (2 persons)

- Kang is angry because he is given only a limited commission; he complains to Emissary Kim. (2 persons)

- Tree-ear tells Ajima what it was like to grow up as an orphan. (2 persons)

- Min tells Tree-ear why he gave him a job after the boy broke his pot. (2 persons)

- Ajima tells Tree-ear why she filled his bowl full of food every evening, even though she didn't know Crane-man yet. (2 persons)

Bibliography of Related Reading

Fiction

Balgassi, Haemi. *Tae's Sonata*. Houghton Mifflin, 1997.

Carpenter, Frances. *Tales of a Korean Grandmother*. C.E. Tuttle Co, 1973.

Choi, Sook Nyul. *Echoes of the White Giraffe*. Houghton Mifflin, 1993.

Choi, Sook Nyul. *Halmoni and the Picnic Ill*. Houghton Mifflin, 1993.

Climo, Shirley. *The Korean Cinderella*. HarperCollins Children's Books, Trophy, 1996.

Gukova, Julia. *The Mole's Daughter: An Adaptation of a Korean Folktale*. Annick Press, 1998.

Heo, Yumi. *The Green Frogs: A Korean Folktale*. Houghton Mifflin Company, 1996.

Holt, Daniel D. *Tigers, Frogs & Rice Cakes: A Book of Korean Proverbs*. Shen's Books, 1998.

Jaffe, Nina. *Older Brother, Younger Brother: A Korean Folktale*. Viking, 1995.

Paek, Min. *Aekyung's Dream*. Children's Book Press, 1988.

Pellegrini, Nina. *Families are Different*. Holiday House, 1991.

Reasoner, Charles. *The Magic Amber: A Korean Legend*. Troll Communications, 1994.

Riordan, James. *Korean Folk-Tales*. Oxford University Press, 2001.

Nonfiction

Kim, Bo-kyung. *Sing 'n' Learn Korean: Introduce Korean with Favorite Children's Songs with Cassette(s)*. Master Communications, Inc., 1997.

Koh, Frances. *Korean Holidays and Festivals*. EastWest Press, 1990.

Landau, Elaine. *Korea*. Children's Press, 1999.

Lee, Lauren. *Korean Americans*. Marshall Cavendish, 1995.

Mcgowen, Tom. *The Korean War*. Franklin Watts, Inc., 1993.

Mcmahon, Patricia. *Chi-Hoon: A Korean Girl*. Boyds Mills Press, 1998.

Stewart, Mark. *Se Ri Pak: The Drive to Win*. Millbrook Press, 2000.

Poetry

Wong, Janet S. *A Suitcase of Seaweed, and Other Poems*. Simon & Schuster, 1996.

Web Sites

Korean Recipes

➤ *http://www.geocities.com/ypmljulia/*

➤ *http://www.recipesource.com/ethnic/asia/korean/indexall.html*

General information about Korea

➤ *http://www.clickasia.co.kr/about.htm*

➤ *http://www.lonelyplanet.com/destinations/north_east_asia/south_korea/*

Answer Key

Page 10

1. He believes he should have told the farmer the moment he saw the rice spilling out.
2. Crane-man tells him that stealing makes him no better than a dog.
3. He was named after a mushroom that grew out of wood without benefit of a parent seed.
4. He went through life with one good leg, standing on it like a crane.
5. The monks brought Tree-ear to Crane-man because of sickness in the monastery, and Tree-ear wanted to stay with him.
6. The potter is a perfectionist and is dramatic while throwing pots, as well.
7. He sees a duck, a melon-like jug, and a lidded box with other boxes inside it.
8. He offers to work for Min in order to pay for the pottery he broke.
9. He is disappointed because he expected to learn to throw pots, and instead he is sent to chop wood.
10. He gets a blister on his hand, has trouble with the heavy cart, and keeps dropping wood from it.

Page 13

Population: 68.3 million
Area: 222,154 km²
Capitol: Seoul
Neighboring countries: China, Japan
Religions: Buddhism, Confucianism, Christianity
Musical instruments: harp, lute, zither, dulcimer, chimes, various drums
Foods: kimchi, rice, noodles, meat, seafood
North Korea and South Korea
Yellow Sea
China
Seoul is south of Korea.
Kaesong is close to the border.

Page 15

1. Tree-ear feels discouraged, as if he's never going to learn to make pottery.
2. Her eyes are bright and soft; they remind him of Crane-man's eyes.
3. He hopes that eventually Min will teach him to make pottery.
4. He and Crane-man will no longer have to look for food in rubbish piles.
5. He feels bad for not helping him catch fish.
6. Min's wife sees that he saves half every day, so she fills the bowl full for his supper.

7. It has an extraordinary color, and the glaze settles into cracks and crevices in an aesthetically pleasing way.
8. He learns that Min takes a long time to make one peace, and his work is expensive. As a younger man, he'd been one of the most successful potters in Ch'ulp'o.
9. He wants a royal commission because of the worthiness of the position and the pay.
10. Accept all reasonable answers.

Page 18

1. new, first quarter (waxing), full, last quarter (waning)
2. one month
3. two months
4. star of the Northern Hemisphere towards which the axis of the earth points
5. They used it to get their bearings and to tell them which way was north.
6. a compass
7. the Mayans
8. The year began in July and was divided into 18 months of 20 days each.
9. an instrument for providing calculations by sliding counters along rods or in grooves
10. a calculator
11. an instrument that shows the time of day by the shadow of a marker on a horizontal surface
12. The shadow pointed to a particular place on the dial, depending on what time it was.

Page 20

1. Kang hides the new inlay technique from the other potters because he wants a royal commission.
2. He wants to make a prunus vase because it is so elegant.
3. They have to sleep in a cold, dark dugout.
4. He was spying on Kang, and he knows it would be deceitful to tell Min.
5. He looks pleased for an instant and then looks cross.
6. He takes time looking at Min's display and recalls a pot used at dinner. He says the work is unmistakable.
7. He recognizes the boy's loyalty and support of his own work.
8. He feels with his fingers that the clay is not yet ready to work with.

Answer Key *(cont.)*

9. He walked toward the monastery, but encountered a fox. He went down the mountain and never came back, and then the monks brought him Tree-ear.
10. He is disgusted by the brown tint of the glaze.

Page 25
1. He asks him to bring his work demonstrating the inlay technique to the palace in Songdo.
2. He can travel with Min's vases to Songdo.
3. She asks him to call her Ajima.
4. Potters' apprentices are the sons of potters. This upsets him because he is an orphan.
5. He is proud and doesn't wish to appear a beggar.
6. He laughs because Tree-ear tries to shame him into working for Ajima.
7. He tells him that people will be his greatest danger, but he must turn to people if he is in need of aid.
8. He encounters a fox. This is significant because of Crane-man's encounter with a fox. Foxes were said to possess evil magic.
9. During the Chinese invasion, women from Puyo jumped off the cliff rather than be captured by the Chinese.
10. They demonstrate the inlay work.

Page 28
1. China
2. The Mongols
3. Japan
4. Japan
5. The United States and the USSR
6. North Korea and South Korea

Page 30
1. The men are hoping he has rice.
2. He is horrified that he failed Min.
3. He wraps clay around the shard's edge, then ties it in his tunic and puts it into his pouch.
4. He remembers that he was born there and wonders if a monk there knows his parents.
5. They think he is a "scrawny scarecrow" with no right to be there.
6. He has seen Min's work before, and he can tell from the shard that Min is a master potter.
7. They don't know how to tell him that Crane-man is dead.
8. A farmer in a cart jostled him on a bridge. Crane-man fell into the cold water, and the shock was too great for his heart.

9. A home and a position as a potter's apprentice.
10. Accept all reasonable answers.

Page 43
Matching
1. Emissary Kim
2. Min
3. Ch'ulp'o
4. Crane-man
5. Ajima
6. Songdo
7. Kang
8. Tree-ear

True or False
1. False
2. True
3. True
4. False
5. False

Short Answer
1. He ate wild plants and food from rubbish piles.
2. They say he takes too long to make one pot and charges too much money.
3. a monkey and a turtle
4. He shows him the shard and tells him what happened with the robbers.
5. The "Thousand Cranes Vase" has intricate inlay work with 46 round medallions. Within every circle, there is a crane. Clouds appear to drift between the medallions with cranes soaring.

Essay
Accept all reasonable answers pertaining to courage.

Page 44
Accept all reasonable and well-supported responses and explanations.

Page 45
Perform the conversations in class. Ask students to respond to conversations by asking the following: "Are the conversations true to the story?" and "Are the characters' words in keeping with their personalities?"